To lovabull,
Happy Birthday from
your
Incorrigabull.

xxx

THE BULL PEN

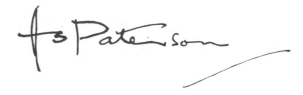

HODDER AND STOUGHTON
AUCKLAND

First published 1969. Reprinted (twice) 1970;
(twice) 1971; (twice) 1972; 1973; (twice) 1974;
1976; 1979.

SBN 340 12903 4

Printed and bound by Dai Nippon Printing Co. (Hong Kong) Ltd.
for Hodder and Stoughton Ltd.,
P.O. Box 3858, Auckland, New Zealand.

FOREWORD

by G.E. Minhinnick, O.B.E., cartoonist for the *New Zealand Herald*, Auckland, since 1930.

Alan Stuart Paterson died on 16 June, 1968.

New Zealanders — and Wellingtonians in particular — will remember him for the first-class daily cartoon news commentaries that he drew every day for 25 years, from 1925 to 1950, for the capital's morning newspaper. Perhaps only a fellow cartoonist can appreciate just how difficult this can be and how superlatively well Alan Paterson did it.

His friends will remember him as a gentle and whimsical philosopher, with a glorious sense of the absurd. They will remember him, too, as an artist and illustrator of distinction and a quiet man.

As for these drawings, I confess it hadn't occurred to me that bulls are figures of fun.

Now I come to think of it, the bull's status on the farm is very funny indeed.

Alan Paterson had already thought of it and this book is the result. It is typical of the universal quality of his humour that these drawings will be enjoyed by everyone, and particularly by farmers, everywhere.

LOVABULL

ENVIABULL

DISREPUTABULL

IRASCIBULL

RELIABULL

FEEBULL

INSUFFERABULL

CONSIDERABULL

INCORRIGABULL

INSATIABULL

INCAPABULL

INESCAPABULL

DEPENDABULL

IMPOSSIBULL

CULPABULL

UNBEATABULL